MORE THAN ORDINARY

abundance:

from Kit's heart

KIT AND DREW COONS

More Than Ordinary Abundance: From Kit's Heart

© 2018 Kit and Drew Coons

ISBN: 978-1-7325783-2-6

Edited by Jayna Richardson
Design: Julie Sullivan (MerakiLifeDesigns.com)

First Edition

Printed in the United States

22 21 20 19 18   1 2 3 4 5

contents

FROM MY HEART
to yours

Many years ago, I started writing in journals. The theme of my journals has always been God's faithfulness. And the title of those journals collectively is *Abundance*. Abundance is defined by Webster's dictionary as a very large amount of something. Words similar in meaning are bounty, plenty, riches, thriving. All of those words describe God's faithfulness to me over my lifetime.

Four years ago, I started writing a monthly blog during a transition time in my life. Old avenues of ministry had come to an end. God challenged me to begin a new avenue of ministry, that of writing (see "Dare to Imagine"). No longer would my words be just for myself, but others could share them. Most of the devotions in this mini-book come from those writings.

My prayer is that in sharing my thoughts, you will be encouraged to rejoice in God's faithfulness—His faithfulness as demonstrated not only in my life but also in yours. And possibly begin your own collection of stories of *Abundance*.

Kit

"I will sing of the Lord's great love forever, with my mouth I will make your faithfulness known through all generations. I will declare that your love stands firm forever, that you have established your faithfulness in heaven itself." (Psalm 89:1-2)

DARE TO
imagine

"See, I am doing a new thing! Now it springs up; do you not perceive it? I am making a way in the wilderness and streams in the wasteland." (Isaiah 43:19)

I love seeing school supplies being stocked in stores each August. All those pencils, crayons, and notebooks. They signal a new beginning, a new year. School supplies seem to have a magical power to cause us to long for the opportunity to have a fresh start.

But having a fresh start means the end of something else. Courage and a significant amount of effort go in to turning from one experience to begin another.

Whenever I'm faced with a new beginning, I think about the movie *You've Got Mail* with Meg Ryan and Tom Hanks. Meg's bookshop—that has been her life since she was a child—is losing money. So much money that she realizes she will have to close the shop.

A friend responds with a bit of wisdom. She tells Meg, "Closing the store is the brave thing to do." Meg replies, "You are such a liar. But thank you." And her friend says, "You are daring to imagine that you could have a different life." I love that. Dare to imagine a different life. That is brave.

God often calls us to dare to imagine, to become aware of new ways to follow Him, to start a new relationship, begin a new type of work, or serve in a new ministry. For me, that came when the ministry Drew and I had for most of our life together changed. Even though we made the choice to go from full time to volunteers, I still felt at a loss. What would I fill my days with? How would life look different going forward? Would the opportunities to make a difference in other people's lives be over? I was having a hard time daring to imagine my life could be different.

As I sought the Lord's wisdom, He gave me the idea of starting a blog. I had written a few articles previously, but I hadn't taken enough time to develop my writing. Now I had the time. My commitment was to write one blog a month for a year. At the end of the first year I sensed that I should continue. Now four years later I am still writing a blog each month as well as other forms of writing.

Is God asking you to be brave? You can be sure that if so, He will give you the strength needed. He can make "*a way in the wilderness and streams in the wasteland.*"

CHANGE YOUR RANT,
change your life

———

"My dear brothers and sisters, take note of this: Everyone should be quick to listen." (James 1:19)

As I listened to Drew, I mouthed along the words he shared — shared rather boldly, I might add. "Don't these people have anything else to do but bother me on the phone? I don't even think they're real people anymore. That's even worse!" I had heard his favorite rant previously.

Of course, the opposite is also true. He can mouth my favorite rant as well. "Every month they bill us something different. I thought we would get away from that when we signed up for their two-year package. But no, every month is higher!" Rant is defined as "to talk in a noisy, excited, or declamatory manner." Yes, that pretty much sums it up.

Thankfully, most of our conversations don't revolve around our favorite rants. That can't be said for everyone. Some relationships are nothing but rants back and forth. Not very pleasant, I'm guessing.

But still, we had both heard each other's rants a little too often lately. So we tried an experiment. "Let's change up our rants. Drew, you express my rant and I'll express yours for a week." Who says a couple that's been married for thirty-seven years doesn't have any fun?

Anticipation filled Monday morning. Drew surprised me by leading off. "If they raise our bill one more time I'm going to . . ." Hearing my favorite rant come out of his mouth was a joy. *Go, Drew, go!* I thought as I enjoyed each word. But as part of the experiment, I couldn't join in. My rant had become his.

After such a wonderful example, I began his rant. "You would think there are more effective ways to get a positive response from someone than by bugging them to death on the phone." His smile from ear to ear seemed to indicate he enjoyed my words. That smile propelled me into a few more minutes of his, now my, rant before I ran out of steam. Our week was off to a great start.

Rants become rants because the person speaking them doesn't think he or she has been heard. So over time, up goes the volume as well as the frequency. Perhaps that sounds familiar.

At this point you might be thinking that we have too much time on our hands or that indeed 37 years of marriage has taken us over the cliff to insanity. But a very important principle can be gleaned from our experiment. By the end of the week, we both felt understood by the other. Previously, we could mouth each other's words, but having expressed the rant for a week we now understood the emotions behind the words. And we discovered that nothing ends a rant faster than the words, "You know, honey, I can really see what you mean. Is there anything I can do to help?" Rant over, message understood.

Drew and I still have lively conversations. But now we're happy to get on the same side when discussing rants about life. Our week taught us that "Change Your Rant, Change Your Life" really is true.

FOREIGNER TO
family

"Consequently, you are no longer foreigners and strangers, but fellow citizens with God's people and also members of his household." (Ephesians 2:19)

The food looked delicious, and I felt starved. But the restaurant in Beijing only provided chopsticks. Drew, with his larger hands, did okay. But my frustration level grew with each morsel I dropped.

Drew and I are blessed with the opportunity to travel. We have spoken for FamilyLife in thirty-nine countries outside the US. Anyone who travels often knows that the glamour quickly fades. But to be halfway around the world and experience a new culture is still a joy to us.

Recently, we took a trip to Asia. The jet lag, constant worry about food-related sickness, and struggle to listen intently through heavy accents challenged us—not to mention my inability to get those chopsticks to cooperate. Added to those challenges was the reality that we didn't look like anyone else. We clearly didn't belong. All who saw us knew.

Touching down back in America brought a surprising feeling. I knew the place. Although I was still far from my home in Arkansas, I instinctively knew how things worked. I no longer felt like a foreigner. I experienced an overwhelming sense of belonging.

The next morning, I read Ephesians 2:19. This scripture contrasts being a foreigner with being a member of God's household. The uncomfortable memory of being a foreigner remained with me. That morning I experienced a new depth of gratitude to be part of God's household. I'm not on the outside, a foreigner, but now a member of a family. What an astonishing thought.

How about you? Are you part of God's household? If so, perhaps you could take a moment right now to think about what a remarkable position you hold.

THE MIRACLE
of tea

"I have hidden your word in my heart that I might not sin against you." (Psalm 119:11)

Tea making has been called many things: a celebration, an ancient rite, and refreshment for the stress of life. The history of tea is long, encompassing many years and countries. In the third century, tea was recorded as being used primarily as a medicine. Much later in the sixteenth century, Portuguese priests and merchants in Lebanon were introduced to tea. In the seventeenth century, tea drinking became popular in Britain. Which eventually brings us to my grandmother. Yes, my grandmother was British.

My grandmother taught me some tea-making secrets, such as knowing how making the tea affects its taste. Traditionally the milk was poured into the cup first to prevent the boiling tea from cracking the delicate porcelain cup. The milk would then add just a bit of a scalded taste, which is much different than if you pour the tea first, then add the milk. In that order the milk does not add a slightly scalded taste. Most American tea drinkers would probably not notice, but those from Britain would.

My day begins with a cup of tea. I always enjoy watching as the tea is immersed in the hot water. Almost magically the water begins to change color. First, there are light amber ribbons of color. Soon they become larger and deeper. The water is infused with the rich brown color and flavor. Every bit of exposed tea is saturated. Slowly, the water becomes something new to be savored and enjoyed.

The miracle of a cup of tea reminds me of the way God's Word changes a life. Like the tea, God's Word penetrates our lives. Slowly at first, as our minds are renewed. Then new ways of thinking give way to new ways of behaving. And ribbons of God's character can be seen in our lives. As each new truth exposes our heart, we become saturated with God's perspective on life. Over a lifetime, like the cup of tea, our lives become something to be savored and enjoyed.

CASTLE
walls

"The weapons we fight with are not the weapons of the world. On the contrary, they have divine power to demolish strongholds." (2 Corinthians 10:4)

Cold wind and rain blew against me on the edge of the wall. My hands shook as I tried to capture with my eyes and camera the huge castle. The sea below roared with waves crashing on rocks. The gray sky complemented the wild wind. I could easily imagine ancient boats tossed upon the rocks below. The interior of the castle welcomed us as we rushed inside. Although cold and dark, the walls sheltered us from the storm. Within those walls, we would be safe.

Drew and I had the privilege to visit the Kyrenia castle in Northern Cyprus. The first historical reference to the castle is in 1191 when King Richard the Lionheart of England captured it by defeating King Isaac Komnenos of Cyprus. As we walked from one incredible room to another, the song "A Mighty Fortress is our God" seemed to be humming in the background. But the music played only in my heart.

Martin Luther wrote the words and melody of that well-loved hymn between 1527 and 1529. Originally written in German, the hymn has been translated into many languages. The words are a paraphrase of Psalm 46. For the psalmist and Martin Luther, the image of a castle conveyed safety and protection—an impregnable fortress.

But in time, with the development of modern weapons, a castle could no longer provide safety. The arrow loops that had allowed those inside to shoot out could then be accurately shot into. The walls that stood so proudly could then be reduced to rubble with cannonballs. Times had changed. The enemy had adjusted their methods and now had the upper hand. What once gave safety and protection no longer did.

While it is true that God is our mighty fortress, I believe He also expects us to adapt to overcome our enemy. Satan will use every method he can to take us captive. Have you noticed any of his new weapons in your life? Perhaps the internet has become an unsecured avenue of information. In the past, putting down a book or turning the channel seemed easier than walking away from all the supposedly "important" information that is now at our fingertips. Have you allowed the enemy to shoot through the arrow loops of your defenses by not setting appropriate boundaries?

Possibly your activities could use a few moments of analysis. Have you maintained your castle walls living by standards that seem as out of date as a castle? Or have you weakened your own walls by choices that aid the enemy in bringing those walls crumbling down? What about your relationships or your finances? The list is long.

We are in a battle. God has provided the weapons we need. But we must take the initiative to adapt to the enemy's new strategies. We cannot stay passively within the castle walls. The way to continue to win the war is to be aware of our enemy's tactics and have a clear way forward. Maybe now would be a good time to begin needed repairs of your castle walls.

Separated

"Love the Lord your God with all your heart and with all your soul and with all your mind . . .Love your neighbor as yourself." (Matthew 22:37, 39)

Drew and I had a layover in London returning from Cyprus, so we took the opportunity to visit the city. We have taken the subways—Brits call it "the tube"—many times and enjoy finding our way around. The flurry of activity underground always amazes this country girl. There are so many people going so many places all at a breakneck speed.

Often when on your way to the platform you can hear the train arrive. People dash to get on the momentarily stopped car. I hesitated to make sure this was the car we wanted. Drew didn't. The doors closed, and he was carried away quicker than my eyes could comprehend. Sheer panic filled my heart. I had been left behind, alone. I wasn't sure of our next stop, I had no way to call him since cell phones don't work underground, and I had no idea what to do. In those situations, we have a family rule: "Go back and wait where you last saw the person."

Our family rule would have worked had I stayed put. But I don't always follow the rules, especially when panicked. I reasoned that Drew would get off at the next stop and wait for me there. So I got on another car, expecting him to be waiting for me. But by the time I got to the next stop, he wasn't there. He was already on his way "back to the last place he saw me." I went back also. The challenge was that going back, the tube drops you off on the opposite platform. No Drew to be found. We each had a couple more rides before we were once again united at the place we had parted. It took some forgiveness, "Oops, I didn't follow the rule," and effort, but we eventually enjoyed spending the rest of the day together.

A couple spiritual parallels come to mind. First, even though Drew and I had been separated, we were still husband and wife. Our separation was temporary. We experience the same principle in our relationship with the Lord. Usually a separation from the Lord is subtler than Drew speeding off in the tube. But we are still God's children even when temporarily separated due to our sin.

Secondly, how do we become united again? In the spiritual realm, we confess the action or attitude that separated us from the Lord and receive His forgiveness. Technically, we are then united. But I don't always feel united so easily. My heart desires to demonstrate that unity.

Many people would suggest spending time in prayer or Bible study. Drew likes to ask God for a project and pursues it. I follow the rule I should have followed underground. "Go back and wait where you last saw the person." There is great joy for me in going back to the basics of my spiritual walk.

"Love the Lord your God with all your heart and with all your soul and with all your mind." And "love your neighbor as yourself." Focusing on loving God and loving my neighbor is what I do. For me, my closest neighbor is Drew. As I seek to serve Drew, I begin to feel my heart united with God.

Again, both forgiveness and effort are needed for restoration of the relationship. Once done, we can then enjoy the rest of the day together.

WISTERIA AND
wounds

"Create in me a pure heart, O God, and renew a steadfast spirit within me." (Psalm 51:10)

Recently I spent several days trimming our wisteria vines. Although I had never enjoyed climbing trees as a kid, I climbed to the top of the ladder and shimmied between the boards that make up our arbor. Some days I felt too scared to climb more than halfway up the ladder. My last day up the ladder I scraped my arm against a rough board. A piece of wood impaled my arm. Blood flowed all over. I was hurt and scared, and down the ladder I went.

Drew was working nearby. We went inside our house to clean my wound. Remembering that still makes me cringe. We scrubbed and scrubbed, but numerous tiny splinters had become embedded in my flesh. Each one had to be pulled out with tweezers. When the tweezers didn't work, we took a safety pin and scraped the wound until we could force the splinters to the surface.

We both knew the time to get the splinters was right then. Even the tiniest sliver of wood could fester and get infected. The wound would then have to be reopened. Cleaning the wound became a long, painful process but had to be done for my own good.

A few days later my heart felt heavy. People vary in their response when emotions interrupt their daily lives. I have learned that getting to the root of my emotions is both effective and efficient. What emotion did I feel? Was I jealous, angry, or self-focused? I then try to confess that root and ask the Lord to change me. In this case, envy was the root.

Envy is unfortunately a recurring characteristic in my heart. I often look at others and desire what they have, and I don't. Opportunities, possessions, even friendships have been on my envy list. In the past after acknowledging my envy, I would feel God's peace. But this time I felt no peace.

Then the Lord reminded me of my arm. "Do you remember the pain cleaning your wound? Do you remember how you had to remove every splinter and then go deeper with the safety pin to dig out each embedded piece?" Looking at my bandaged arm, this wasn't hard to recall. "That is what I'm desiring to do in your heart, Kit. There are some deep splinters of envy that have festered. They need to come out. But they won't come out the usual way. Some digging needs to be done. Will you allow me to clean this wound?"

I'd like to say that trusting God made His work easier to accept. But that wasn't true. There was a deep examination of my heart, sadness, and confession as the Lord removed the embedded splinters of envy. And boundaries in my thought life needed to be put in place so I wouldn't allow envy to become embedded in my heart again.

My arm is no longer bandaged, and my heart is no longer heavy. Both have experienced God's healing. In some ways, the healing came differently, yet in other ways much the same. Perhaps the Lord has been trying to remove a splinter from your heart. Will you take the first step to remove the splinter? The process will be painful, but it will be for your own good.

HOW DO I LOVE YOU?
let me count the ways

———

"For I am convinced that neither death nor life, neither angels nor demons, neither the present nor the future, nor any powers, neither height nor depth, nor anything else in all creation, will be able to separate us from the love of God that is in Christ Jesus our Lord." (Romans 8:38-39)

As children, many of us played a French game created in the 1800s. A daisy is used to tell us whether someone loves us or not. "He loves me" is spoken and a petal is plucked off. "He loves me not," and another petal is plucked off. The last petal reveals the answer. There is no truth in the game. But the game exposes our deep need, even as children, to be loved.

Young or old, we all have the desire to be loved. Our hearts cry out "Am I loved?" God, having created our hearts, knows our need. In Romans 8:38-39, we read His gracious answer.

These verses tell us about our new life in Christ and our future glory. Romans 8:37 encourages us to be more than conquerors and to live our lives as Christ would. Not easy, but we are also given the foundation of our strength in the verses that follow. Those verses seem to shout the fact that God loves us! "Everyone listen! God loves me!" Not only are we loved, but also nothing can separate us from that love.

When you see a flower today, be reminded you are loved. Live in confidence knowing nothing will happen today or any day to separate you from God's love.

THERE WILL ALWAYS BE RATS
on the carport

"I was given a thorn in my flesh, a messenger of Satan, to torment me." (2 Corinthians 12:7b)

Driving in our truck to get a load of wood chips for mulch in our garden, we smelled something not quite right. Our truck was very old, and unusual smells were just part of the experience. So we didn't pay much attention. However, billows of black smoke filling the cab convinced us something was wrong. I yelled at Drew to pull over. He shouted back, "Let's go just a bit farther." To which I replied . . . well, no need to repeat that.

Once orange and red spikes of fire showed, Drew did pull over. We ran for our lives. To our surprise, we saw a new fire station just across the street. The sight of the fire truck, lights and sirens on, coming across the street gathered a crowd. We all watched as they put the fire out. After looking at the damage, the firemen gave us the phone number of a wrecker service to haul away the beyond-repair truck.

That experience will always be remembered as the beginning of learning a principle we call "There will always be rats on the carport." Yes, rats. You city dwellers most likely think I am telling a "whopper" of a story, but my fellow country dwellers know different. Rats had made a nest in our truck and chewed the wiring. We don't know which of those wires caused the fire, but we know the rodent who did. A week later when our Corolla wouldn't start, we lifted the hood to find a new rat nest, chewed wiring, and the rat himself.

We rode in a tow truck to the dealership, finding out later that a rat had come along for the ride. He frightened the mechanics, who left the destructive rodent in the car to gnaw away while they presented us with a $7,000 repair estimate. That night I lay awake while an expensive new rental car sat in the very spot that the rats had done their damage, twice.

Unwelcome visitors show up in everyone's lives. The issue is how we will deal with them. Do we allow the rats on the carport to continue their destruction? Will we allow anxieties to take away our sleep at night? By God's grace, we calmly investigated our alternatives. A different mechanic agreed to fix our car for $305. Next, we returned the expensive rental car, safe from any rodent damage, and started a campaign to drive away the rats. That's not so easy. They still visit our carport each night. Our car and a replacement truck sit with the hoods open and bags of rat-repellant mothballs on the engine block and each tire. Rats like to climb, you know.

The rats technically are not a "thorn in our flesh," but they definitely tormented us and still do. Our lives will always have interruptions by destructive forces—"rats on the carport." Fortunately, God gave us the ability to logically, if not completely calmly, think through our options. Step by step we trusted Him and did what we could do. Our final step was to put this "thorn in the flesh" in perspective. The rats were not the biggest challenge we have ever faced. Once we did that, we could then get a good night's sleep.

A LOOK BEHIND BEFORE
moving ahead

"These stones are to be a memorial to the people of Israel forever." (Joshua 4:7b)

When I was a new Christian, a friend suggested journaling and gave me my first book of empty pages. The inscription on the cover is, "Today's Happy Moments, Tomorrow's Happy Memories." The first page is dated April 18th, 1974.

My now eighteen completed journals are all sizes and shapes, including the one written in this week. Each one is a step back into a time I once lived. The pages are filled with experiences that, like stones one by one, build a memorial of remembrance to the Lord.

Long before me, the children of Israel built memorials to the Lord. God's instruction to them was to build a pillar of stones to serve as a memorial of His work in their lives. Although my journals are not very tall in stature, they do have a wealth of God's workings with one of His children.

Another way of building memorials of remembrance is by choosing a scripture each year on which to concentrate. In 1996, someone challenged me to begin this practice. Twenty-two verses remind me of how the verse chosen each January became just what I needed for the journey of that year. The verses vary greatly in subject, but the common thread is the effect of God's Word on a life.

Might I challenge you to do the same? Perhaps choose a verse that emphasizes a character quality you would like to develop in your life, or a promise that will give you courage as you anticipate the highs and lows ahead. As years pass, your verses will build a memorial of remembrance to the Lord as you review the impact they have had on your life.

This year Drew has chosen our verse. "Finally, brothers and sisters, whatever is true, whatever is noble, whatever is right, whatever is pure, whatever is lovely, whatever is admirable — if anything is excellent or praiseworthy — think about such things." (Philippians 4:8) I look forward to the process of training my thoughts to focus on good things.

forgiveness

"Bear with each other and forgive one another if any of you has a grievance against someone. Forgive as the Lord forgave you." (Colossians 3:13)

"Do you remember what you tell everyone at the conference about how to handle conflict?" I confronted Drew. "No 'you' statements, stick to one issue, don't bring up the past, no personal attacks."

Not surprisingly, that didn't get a good response. But then, I didn't respond well either when I heard Drew say, "Excuse me. What about how you tell everyone to give a blessing for an insult? I don't think your accusation was a blessing."

Drew and I have had the privilege to teach biblical principles of relationships for many years. Undoubtedly, teaching those principles has enriched our marriage. But there have also been times when we wished we had never heard those principles. Knowing and doing are two vastly different things. I had been caught by my own words, and there is nothing worse. Well, actually there is. When we refuse to look at our behavior, admit our fault, and extend forgiveness, the consequences are far greater.

Living in harmony together is no small task. And the challenge is not limited to one country or people. Part of the joy Drew and I receive from international travel is the opportunity to see the universality of marriage. Because of different cultures, marriage may look different. But men's and women's hearts are the same wherever you go. We all struggle with how to live in harmony with other people, even those we love.

After one time of disharmony in our relationship, Drew came to me to ask forgiveness. But as he thought about his words, he said, "I've actually come to express regret. I know you have already forgiven me." He was right. I had forgiven him shortly after the words were spoken because I have learned that to not forgive only hurts me.

God does the same thing. His forgiveness was made available to us when He died for our sins. When I come to Him after I have chosen to sin, I come to express my regret. I know He has already forgiven me. My sin cannot take His forgiveness away. Nevertheless, expressing our regret to another person or to God is the way to restore our relationship.

Forgiveness is the glue that holds any relationship together. In our relationship with God, His forgiveness makes the relationship possible. In our relationships with others, forgiveness also makes the relationship possible. Is there someone who needs your forgiveness? Well, really is there someone you need to forgive for your own good? Now would be the perfect time to extend your forgiveness.

Research has shown that the ability to forgive is the foremost reason a person will have a happy life. I agree.

GARDENING
101

"It [faith] is like a mustard seed, which a man took and planted in his garden. It grew and became a tree, and the birds perched in its branches." (Luke 13:19)

Oh, for the Garden of Eden! Adam and Eve had no idea what they had to give up, until afterwards. Then they knew, as do we. But as the saying goes, "hope springs eternal." So every spring—no pun intended—Drew and I demonstrate our hope by preparing, digging, and planting our little bit of earth.

Looking at the freshly planted garden is the spring equivalent of the beginning of football season. Every team thinks that this will be the year they bring home the trophy. And Drew and I dream of bringing in crops grander than last year.

The English peas came first, then the asparagus, and raspberries. The blackberries arrived next in abundance. We ate blackberries, gave blackberries away, and juiced blackberries to make jelly.

The blackberries kept coming whether we were ready or not. And ready I was not. I complained about all the blackberries. I didn't appreciate their gift of abundance. As quickly as they came, the harvest was over. Now I wish I could enjoy more blackberries.

Life can be the same. We don't realize the fleeting nature of the season. We don't acknowledge the abundance around us or focus on the delight of what we are experiencing. Often Drew will stop me to say, "Kit, enjoy the moment." I need his reminder to not miss what is right in front of me.

Next the garden produced red potatoes, corn, cucumbers, beans, peppers, and tomatoes. They are all amazing in their ability to give lavish fruit from such a small start. But the sunflowers amazed me the most. Tilting my head up to see them, I was filled with wonder. How could there be so much potential in that tiny seed?

The Bible says faith like a mustard seed can move mountains. I have never literally moved a mountain. But I have seen mountains of problems, grief, and seemingly irresolvable situations moved when I placed my small seed of faith in God. The sunflowers encourage me that God can do much more than I imagine.

Admiring the transformation of seed, sunlight, and water, I pause to reflect on God's transforming work in my life. How about you? Do you need to slow down to enjoy the season? Or perhaps you need to be encouraged that God really can do more than you imagine. His gardening tools may be different, but the result is just as extraordinary.

EMBRACING
imperfection

"There is no fear in love. But perfect love drives out fear, because fear has to do with punishment. The one who fears is not made perfect in love." (1 John 4:18)

If you let your fingers do the walking—and I don't mean through the yellow pages—but rather on Google, you will discover much talk about "embracing imperfection." "Seventeen Affirmations to Embrace Imperfection," "The Art of Embracing Imperfections," and "The Gifts of Imperfection" top the list of articles. Since we all deal with imperfections, many words have been written on the subject.

The articles encourage releasing the dream of perfection by lowering your standards, giving yourself a break, and looking realistically at yourself. After making a careful assessment, one can move forward with a different perspective and handle imperfections with newfound confidence. Some of that is probably good advice. However, I recently had an experience with a slightly different takeaway.

One of my joys is gift giving. The goal is to give a gift that says, *I know who you are, and I love who you are.* I knew that one of my niece's favorite verses was "Strength and dignity are her clothing, and she smiles at the future." (Proverbs 31:25, NASB) So I thought I would calligraphy and frame the verse. Perfecting my calligraphy skills consumed many pieces of paper. Because the deadline fast approached, I had to finally settle on one.

My niece loved the gift. The message had been conveyed and goal accomplished. A few days later my sister gently pointed out that I had misspelled the word "strength." She wanted me to know so I could replace the verse, if I chose to. Which brought new thoughts on imperfection.

Yes, I could make another calligraphy to replace the imperfect one. But I wondered if leaving it imperfect didn't carry a deeper message. Our imperfections are the very things that bring us to God. And our imperfections give us the opportunity to experience the comfort of God's grace. Rather than being something to over-look, imperfections drive me to the One who loves me just as I am. I shared my thoughts with my niece and let her decide what I should do. She kept the original version. Smart girl.

How are you doing handling your imperfections? Do they drive you away from God, or do they drive you to Him? Thankfully, God doesn't require something we are not—perfect—but His love in our imperfections is perfect.

OVERCAST
skies

"Direct me in the path of your commands, for there I find delight." (Psalm 119:35)

Some don't like overcast days, but I enjoy them. The gray sky softens the colors in my house and brings a feeling of coziness. My instinct is to cuddle up. Slowly I begin to feel surrounded, as if in a cocoon. The clouds lull me into their stillness.

Then abruptly the clouds leave and allow the sun to shine. The sun is like a beacon after the grayness, bringing revelation. The light exposes what the clouds did not. As I see the dust on my furniture or the marks on the floor I hadn't moments before, I often wish for the grayness to return. Where did all the dust and dirt come from?

Sin can have the same characteristics. We often feel an element of coziness with sin, a familiarity that allows us to cuddle up with wrongdoing. Sin lulls us with its subtleness. We are quick to underestimate how each decision we make influences the rest of our decisions. One wrong decision often leads easily to another. Much like a blanket over our heart, sin keeps us from seeing clearly.

But thankfully, the sun comes out. The Holy Spirit convicts us. He uses the light of God's Word to expose our cloudy thinking. At times we might need more than God's Word to convince us of our poor decision-making. Others are also affected by our actions.

God is ready to help us examine the areas of sin that have become cozy. And He is ready to give us the power to continue to walk in the light.

AN
illusion

"Teach us to number our days, that we may gain a heart of wisdom." (Psalm 90:12)

Drew and I sat in the auditorium waiting for the video to begin. The first thing we always do when visiting a national park visitor center is watch the introductory video. We had come to Yellowstone to celebrate our thirty-third wedding anniversary. The room darkened, and the screen filled with light. We watched in amazement as the grandeur of Yellowstone came alive. The photographer must have patiently waited for hours to record the animals, weather patterns, and light on the mountains of the park. The images overwhelmed us.

As we watched, a narrative voice said almost in a whisper, "Our earth appears to be so solid. We see no movement daily. But that's not true. The earth is never still. Permanence is an illusion."

Those words captured my thoughts. The earth does appear to be solid and without movement. The video continued to show the constant movement of the park. Never still. And as I watched, I realized that my marriage also seems to have no movement daily. But like the earth, marriage is always moving either toward unity or toward isolation. Yellowstone with its constant change is an apt comparison for a marriage relationship.

At times our marriages, or any other relationships, seem to be solid, steady, and immovable. So much so that on occasion I have taken those relationships for granted, putting them on auto-pilot assuming all will flow along nicely without any effort on my part.

But that doesn't last for long. A challenge of some kind interrupts the flow, making me realize that I'm losing ground. An unkind word, a misunderstood emotion, or even a sense of isolation can bring me back to the reality that, like Yellowstone, there is always movement in human relationships. They are never still.

I'm reminded that taking the time to listen, learning how to resolve conflict, and putting each other first are worthy goals in a marriage relationship. I need to pause long enough to become aware that our relationship is moving one way or the other and invest in it with determination, time, and humility.

For most of our 37 years together, Drew and I have desired and been encouraged to be aware of this constant motion and work toward unity. We have had the privilege of encouraging others to do the same. And when you tell others how to make marriage work, you had better be sure yours works—definitely a motivating factor.

How about you? Do you have relationships in your life that need some attention? Thinking that relationships will take care of themselves without continued investment is an illusion. Neither the earth nor our relationships are ever stagnant. Which way are yours moving?

Before we left home, we received an anniversary card from my sister. She made this comment in it: "You are reaping the benefits of all your hard work on your marriage." How true that is.

A
glimpse

"What no eye has seen, what no ear has heard, and what no human mind has conceived—the things God has prepared for those who love him." (1 Corinthians 2:9)

At the end of one summer, we experienced a lot of excitement. Friends and neighbors all around felt the anticipation. Our weatherman gave us a hint of our future: a weekend with cooler temperatures and lower humidity was on its way. Now, that might not sound like much. But at the end of an Arkansas summer, this was a dream come true.

Our summers are always hot. But when Keith, our weatherman, started saying we were going to have cooler air from Canada, we all started counting the days. Many made plans to enjoy the outdoors. Just as promised, we had two glorious days of lows in the 60s and highs in the 80s. Those days were promises that fall would eventually arrive.

Webster's Dictionary defines a glimpse as "a momentary or partial view, a brief or quick look." And a quick look our two days were. As if a sponge, I tried to absorb the coolness. We hardly had enough time to turn off the air conditioning and open all the windows. But the cooler days had done their job. They reminded us of better days to come. They refreshed our hearts. They gave us hope.

Perhaps because the weather felt so heavenly I realized that a glimpse of heaven could have the same effect. Intentional thoughts of heaven remind us of better days to come. There is more to my life than it seems. "When I consider your heavens, the work of your fingers, the moon and the stars, which you have set in place, what is mankind that you are mindful of them, human beings that you care for them?" (Psalm 8:3-4)

Thoughts of heaven refresh our hearts. They change our perspective. "And I heard a loud voice from the throne saying, 'Look! God's dwelling place is now among the people, and he will dwell with them. They will be his people, and God himself will be with them and be their God. He will wipe every tear from their eyes. There will be no more death or mourning or crying or pain, for the old order of things has passed away.' " (Revelation 21:3-4)

Thoughts of heaven give us hope. There is a worthy end ahead. "Then the King will say to those on his right, 'Come, you who are blessed by my Father; take your inheritance, the kingdom prepared for you since the creation of the world.' " (Matthew 25:34)

I cannot control the weather, but I can control how often I think of heaven. God's Word is ready to encourage our hearts as often as we need. Recently, Bill, a friend of ours, reminded me, "Heaven is our home. This is a field trip."

FOR THE LOVE OF
the game

"Whatever you do, work at it with all your heart, as working for the Lord, not for human masters, since you know that you will receive an inheritance from the Lord as a reward. It is the Lord Christ you are serving." (Colossians 3:23-24)

A new football season always brings hope. Any team can walk away a champion. Each year a new slate is given to every team; so refreshing, so exciting, so comforting.

When football fans think of someone who loved the game, Brett Favre comes to mind. Sure, he wanted to win. He enjoyed the clean slate each year. But his love of playing the game drove him. He just wanted to play football.

I recently watched a program about Brett's career. The program mentioned that Brett broke every football record. When I shared that with Drew, he said that while Brett was truly an amazing player, longevity also figured into those stats. He had made an interesting point.

Longevity is defined as long life, long duration, or continuance. That was Brett in football. Granted, many think it would have been better for his legacy if he had gone out while still on top. But he loved the game too much. He would play for anyone who let him.

Two thoughts come to my mind. The first question I ask myself is how much do I love to play the game? The game I'm referring to is our service to the Lord. Do I love the Lord enough to serve in whatever way He asks? Is my joy in serving rather than in winning? Or do I just want the service that helps my reputation—service positions that make my stats look good?

And secondly, will I stay in the game when the opportunities for service become less than they may have been previously? Or will I leave the game while still on top so people will remember me in a more favorable way?

What we remember about Brett is not how many games he won, but how much he loved to play. I would like to be remembered the same way. Not how I served, but that I loved to serve.

PARSLEY, SAGE, ROSEMARY,
and thyme

"Now thanks be to God who always leads us in triumph in Christ, and through us diffuses the fragrance of His knowledge in every place." (2 Corinthians 2:14, NKJV)

I love to grow herbs. My garden has several kinds. They add texture, color, and fragrance. I love to pick the leaves, crush them in between my fingers, and breathe deeply. Wonderful aromas.

A favorite recipe of mine is "rosemary sea salt focaccia bread." I made a loaf recently for guests. Making bread is a feast for olfactory senses. But when you add herbs, you are in for a treat.

I start by going to the rosemary bush and cutting the long, straight spires. Once I cut a handful, I strip the tender leaves.

The kitchen begins to fill with the wonderful smell of rosemary. Then I chop the leaves. The more I chop, the stronger the smell.

Next, I stir the rosemary pieces into the dough and set the dough aside to rise. The bowl is covered with a cloth, but a faint smell of rosemary still comes through. The odor promises something special soon to be experienced.

A second rising of the dough occurs in a flat jellyroll pan. I brush olive oil over the surface and then sprinkle on sea salt. Into the oven the dough goes, and out comes an amazing smell. What a fragrance! The bread is aromatic, but the rosemary is overwhelming. Going beyond the kitchen, the whole house has been filled with the earthy, rich, slightly acidic odor of that treasure from the garden. You might even recognize the smell if you walked in while the bread was baking. My stomach responds with instant hunger.

As I was enjoying the smell of the baking bread, 2 Corinthians 2:14 came to mind. Paul referred to captives brought home after a military campaign. He saw himself marching in that parade as a new captive of God because of Christ.

The fragrance of incense preceded the parade. Paul illustrated the knowledge of Christ as the incense. The fragrance of that knowledge spread from those who had been taken captive. The knowledge filled Paul's life and heart with the desire to pass it on to all who would listen.

I wondered if my life was as fragrant. Can others see the knowledge of Christ in the way I live my life? Does my life give forth an unmistakable fragrance? Do others become hungry for the knowledge of God after spending time with me?

As I took the bread out of the oven, our guests arrived. Stepping into the house, they immediately commented on the wonderful aroma. We sat down to eat and passed the bread. While Drew gave thanks for our meal, I also whispered my thanks for the reminder that my life could be a fragrance for Christ.

contentment

———

"But godliness with contentment is great gain." (1 Timothy 6:6)

Drew is an animal lover. Dogs, cats, deer, Canada geese, river otters, ducks, and fish have all been a part of our lives. Many are wild and are our temporary guests. Others—the cats in particular—are strays that found our country home. Their diverse personalities and traits are an endless delight to Drew. For me, not as much, but Drew is convinced animals can teach us a lot.

His favorite, Joey—a Russian Blue male cat—demonstrated calmness to me daily. So calm that I sometimes wondered if he was still alive. What I might describe as lazy, Drew described completely differently. He says Joey was content—content with his home, his food, and his life. The word content means satisfied. That's a great picture of our Joey. He was a very satisfied cat.

The Bible study *Becoming a Woman Whose God Is Enough* by Cynthia Heald has a chapter on contentment. Cynthia also defines contentment as satisfied but with a bit of a twist. She went on to say, "Satisfied not because something is in sufficient supply, but satisfied with whatever is available." She gave an example of an unexpected and unwanted event that I could strongly relate to.

Cynthia and her husband, Jack, were traveling. Because of cancelled flights they found themselves in an airport for the night. Looking around, the only bed available was the carpet. She prayed and asked the Lord to make her content with the bed He had supplied. It probably wasn't the best night of sleep she's ever had, but she was content—amazing to me, as someone who has spent a night or two in airports not nearly as contented.

As I reflected on Cynthia's definition of contentment, Joey came to mind. I realized he too was content with what was available. He trusted us to give him what he needed, trusted that we wanted his best. When I remember Joey, I wonder if I demonstrate that same kind of contentment. Hebrews 13:5 says, "And be content with what you have." Thoughts of Joey help me reach toward that worthy goal.

WHAT GIVES YOU
joy?

"Let the fields be jubilant, and everything in them; let all the trees of the forest sing for joy." (Psalm 96:12)

One year my sister gave me a plaque that said, "Joy is the most infallible sign of the presence of God." She didn't mean the gift to be negative, but I felt convicted from the first moment I saw the words.

Many scriptures talk about joy. Psalm 96:12 stated above is my favorite. I love imagining that day. Also, "Surely you have granted him unending blessings and made him glad with the joy of your presence" (Psalm 21:6) and "Restore to me the joy of your salvation and grant me a willing spirit, to sustain me." (Psalm 51:12)

Perhaps the most well-known joy verse is, "But the angel said to them, 'Do not be afraid. I bring you good news that will cause great joy for all the people.' " (Luke 2:10) God wants us to experience joy. He went to great lengths to secure joy for us. But if you are like me, there have probably been times in your life when you were less than joyful. What should we do when joy is far from our hearts?

Many would suggest that we pray, asking God to change our hearts. Joy is one of the fruits of the Spirit. Others would say we should fill our minds with scriptures that focus on joy. These are wonderful suggestions. In addition, I would add that we take an active responsibility for our joy. We need to know what gives us joy. Then we can pursue joy as we seek God.

Years ago, a friend gave me some advice. She suggested I do something creative when my heart felt joyless. By either finishing a project or beginning a new one, I realized that God gave me joy when using my time in a creative way.

Drew receives joy by walking through our home and looking at the pictures of the places God has taken us. Those pictures remind him of having trusted God. As he focuses on the different places he has seen God at work, joy comes naturally.

But for that to happen, he had to first realize that the pictures could give him joy. He had to select, print, frame, and find space for them on our already-crowded walls. He had to know his heart, what gives his heart joy, and take action. He is a wise man.

After 45 years, that plaque from my sister still hangs in our home as a reminder. How about you? Do you know what gives your heart joy? If not, take a few moments right now. Search your heart. What steps can you take to build joy into your life?

My hope for you is the same as a friend shared with me. "May the Lord give you the joy that surpasses your expectation."

scars

"He heals the brokenhearted and binds up their wounds."
(Psalm 147:3)

Drew acquired a new scar recently. Before his surgery I tried to provide assurance by reminding him of my own scars. I have what is called a bikini scar on my abdomen from surgery when I was a teenager. After the surgery I learned I had been born with one kidney and two uteruses. I also learned that having children would be a challenge.

My lip has a scar from falling and hitting a sidewalk on a morning run. And many years later, I added a scar across the right side of my chest from breast cancer. Those scars, although still seen, have not affected my overall health. Sometimes I forget they are even there.

We envisioned Drew's scar being from his ear to his collarbone, but the scar isn't quite that long and has healed nicely. God created our bodies with such amazing capabilities.

A scar is defined as a mark left on the skin after an injury or wound has healed. Physical scars are one thing, but there are other scars, scars of the heart. During Drew's medical challenges we had time to think about those as well.

I'm not sure there is a way to live life without acquiring wounds of the heart. Some small and some larger, they also leave scars. God has designed our hearts as well as our bodies to be able to heal from the wounds of life. But we have a part to play in the healing. Drew was careful to keep his incision clean. He protected it from harm and rested his whole body knowing that healing takes energy. We seem to instinctively know what it takes to help our bodies heal, but what about our hearts? Do we keep them clean by extending forgiveness? Do we protect them from harm by choosing to focus on the positive? And when ready, do we have the energy to move forward?

Possibly now would be a good time to look at your own wounds. Do you have wounds of the heart that haven't quite healed? Do they affect your emotional health? Are there unhealed wounds that—instead of being almost forgotten—are the first things that come to mind?

Drew's recent medical procedures came completely unexpectedly and frightened us, but we used the opportunity to look at all of our wounds. We realized that the wounds of our hearts have healed also. Yes, there are scars left on our hearts, but the injuries that caused them don't dominate our lives. Jehovah Rapha, God our healer, has been at work.

THANKFUL
goodbyes

"Like apples of gold in settings of silver is a word spoken in right circumstances." (Proverbs 25:11, NASB)

Thankful goodbyes? Are goodbyes ever thankful?

All of us have lost loved ones. Death touches everyone and usually comes in one of two ways: a long, lingering illness, or suddenly with no warning. Several friends had recently experienced the sudden loss of a loved one. Completely unexpected—they had no time to say "goodbye."

The thought of missing the opportunity to say goodbye to Drew upset me. Losing the love of my life would be hard enough without thinking that I didn't get to tell him goodbye. So I decided to tell him goodbye. No, he isn't sick. No, I don't have any premonitions. I just didn't want to wait and possibly not have the opportunity to tell him goodbye. So I sat Drew down and told him all that was in my heart. I said goodbye.

I tell Drew I love him daily, but the focus of my goodbye was different. I had spent days before thinking about my life—what my life might have been without Drew and what it is because of him. My goodbye centered on how my life was radically changed because of him. I had lots of examples. I was specific. My thankfulness for the part he has played in my life was the theme. Mine was a thankful goodbye.

But, of course, our spouses are not the only ones who should receive our thanks. Family members, friends, teachers, co-workers, neighbors, any and all who have had an influence for good in our lives should be thanked.

Why not spend a few moments thinking about your life and those who have influenced it positively? Expressing your thanks in person is always best. If that's not possible, send a note. Either way, your heart will be comforted knowing you have not left your thanks unsaid.

JUNIPER
breeze

———

"I will repay you for the years the locusts have eaten—the great locust and the young locust, the other locusts and the locust swarm." (Joel 2:25)

The smell overwhelmed me as I rubbed the lotion into my hands. Juniper Breeze has been my favorite since the first time I used the lotion. Twenty-one years later, the smell instantly transported me to that first experience.

Shortly after communism fell, Drew and I visited Bucharest, Romania. A typical winter day of cold and gray skies greeted us on our first visit to Eastern Europe. As we walked the city I said, "This looks like Western Europe, only in a nightmare." Buildings of beautiful architecture stood neglected, colorless, and un-welcoming.

As we walked into the home of our American hosts, I felt amazed. Like Alice stepping through the looking glass, I became overwhelmed and a bit confused. Their home surrounded us with color, warmth, and beauty.

We settled in to enjoy their hospitality with a whistling teapot, cookies, and conversation. Later I found the bottle of Juniper Breeze lotion in our guest room. Opening the bottle, I smelled the scent for the first time. To me it encapsulated my experience: the desolation of the city compared to the bright, alive joy of their home.

Before I received Christ, my life resembled the neglected, colorless city — broken down from years of wrong choices. But like stepping into the missionary's home, years of making biblical choices have brought color, life, and joy. The effects of obedience have slowly replaced the effects of devastation. What a redemptive God! Not only does He give us a new life, but He also redeems our years of rebellion.

eliminations

"Therefore, since we are surrounded by such a great cloud of witnesses, let us throw off everything that hinders and the sin that so easily entangles. And let us run with perseverance the race marked out for us." (Hebrews12:1)

Drew and I have had the privilege of speaking in thirty-nine foreign countries. Usually international ministry requires speaking through a translator. We have learned that skill and passed it on to others. The most important tip is that you only have half the allotted time. Your translator must repeat what you've said. You must eliminate half of your words to allow the translator time. Much thought goes into deciding what needs to be said and what doesn't to speak effectively.

Some aspects of writing are similar. Thoughts become ideas, ideas become words, and suddenly my computer screen is filled. But again, effective writing has limits. A magazine article allows 1,200 words, a summary 700 words, or this devotion 400 words or less. That may seem like a lot, but words pile up quickly. The real skill in writing is the elimination of words. Does the meaning get lost in my abundance of words?

The word count button on my computer gets a workout as I delete words to clarify my point. Right now, my word count is 195, and I haven't even started to make my point. Or have I?

Living life is much like speaking through a translator or writing well. What do our lives say to others? Is our message clear? Or are our lives a muddle of activities with no real point?

Each of us makes daily decisions that shape our lives. We decide what to keep, what to let go. Most of us are not deciding between good and bad but rather between good and best. Knowing the difference between the good we can do and the best is a start. Then we must ask ourselves how can we do more than just live our lives? How can we invest them?

Speaking through a translator and writing effectively are skills of refinement, eliminating the unnecessary for the necessary. I've heard living life well is also a skill—one that takes constant refinements to make sure we are giving our best to what matters the most. When I look at my life, there are always areas that can be eliminated; the process of refinement never ends.

FOG AND *faith*

———

"Now faith is confidence in what we hope for and assurance about what we do not see." (Hebrews 11:1)

Recently I enjoyed being in California. My sister and mom invited me to join them in the San Francisco area right across the bay from the city. Views of the city, the Golden Gate Bridge, and Sausalito amazed us. That is, when we could see them.

Depending on the fog, you could either see the city or you could see nothing. There would be no hint of any city anywhere in that direction. Both the Golden Gate Bridge and Sausalito appeared or disappeared the same way. Their existence seemed to depend on the weather.

As I watched this happen repeatedly, it reminded me of faith. Like San Francisco, faith can be seen at times but can also be completely hidden.

My life has experienced both. When I pray following God's leading, you could say my faith is hidden, although it still exists.

There are other times, like in writing this devotional, when my faith is more visible. Beginning writing was like looking at the fog that makes San Francisco completely disappear. I had no clear picture of what was ahead, no idea of how to start, no idea where this adventure would take me.

As I wrote I tried to bring my faith out of the fog into the clear and allow God to be glorified by sharing His work in my heart and life. Hopefully my writing shows that my faith exists when it can be seen and even when not seen.

encouragement

"Therefore encourage one another and build each other up, just as in fact you are doing." (1Thessalonians 5:11)

I had almost completed my list of errands with one last pickup to make. The man in the store cheerfully served me. Since we were the only ones in the store, I asked about the pictures on the wall that told the history of the company. He told me the story of each picture as if turning pages in his own personal photo album.

The next week I returned with Drew. The man who had served me previously remembered me and served me again. Drew and I turned to leave. But before we did, I mentioned to the store manager the excellent service I had received on my first visit. I made sure the manager knew the person who had served me was doing a very good job and was in a large part the reason I returned.

In the car, Drew mentioned the words I had shared with the manager. He both noticed and praised me for taking the opportunity to encourage someone for a job well done. The words I had spoken to the store manager took a short time to say. But, by the look on the face of the man who had served me, their impact was much larger.

I was reminded of the power of encouragement. In this case, both the man in the store and I were encouraged by another person's words. Encouragement is like that. Once given it grows to bless many. Whenever I notice someone doing something right, I have a perfect opportunity to use my words for encouragement.

LOVE YOUR
enemies

———

"When the perishable has been clothed with the imperishable, and the mortal with immortality, then the saying that is written will come true: 'Death has been swallowed up in victory.' " (1 Corinthians 15:54)

Recently I have been reading *Devotional Classics* edited by Richard J. Foster and James Bryan Smith. These two men gathered selections from fifty-two authors' works. The authors' dates of birth range from 331 to 1935. The devotionals are an impressive collection of ideas and thoughts that goes beyond my often-limited view of Christianity.

George A. Buttrick, who lived from 1892-1980, laid out several suggestions for prayer. As in many suggestions for prayer, he cites Jesus' command to "love our enemies." I stopped to think about who my enemies might be. I was a bit surprised at my conclusion.

There are people no doubt who don't like me. I am far from a perfect person. But since they have not made themselves known, I didn't list them as enemies. I thought further, and most of the challenges I have that could be considered enemies had one theme. Each challenge involved the passing of time. Time is my worst enemy.

I know that doesn't sound new or original, but should time be my enemy? I certainly view time that way. Part of my view stems from our culture. Americans do not respect age. Our culture revolves around the young. But more important, each year brings challenges to the health of my loved ones and my own health. This earthly tent is showing some real wear. That is reality, and yet even as my heart longs for life to continue, my heart also longs for eternity.

El Olam is the name of God that speaks to His eternity, the Everlasting God. And in Ecclesiastes 3:11 we read, "He has also set eternity in the human heart." My longing for eternity is God-given. Thinking of my future as a countdown to a painful and possibly lonely end needs to change. Instead, I need to view my future as a countdown to the beginning of life as God intended.

Yes, there are going to be challenges along the way as I say goodbye to those I love, and my body continues to slowly wear out and finally no longer functions. But I need to embrace the passage of time as gain, not loss. Each challenge is a step closer to, not further away from, the fulfillment of my longing for eternity. In eternity, time will no longer be my enemy.

belonging

"My Father's house has many rooms; if that were not so, would I have told you that I am going there to prepare a place for you?" (John 14:2)

Drew and I had returned from a two-week mission assignment for FamilyLife. We enjoyed a wonderful time of worship, learning, and trusting God. To label the trip a spiritual high would not be an exaggeration. We trained new people, experienced a new culture, and began a work that we hoped would continue to influence many lives after we left.

Returning home, tiredness, jet lag, and feeling the pressure of being away for so long greeted us. I also have difficulty transitioning from one place to the next. Amid feeling sad and a little lonely, I wished we were still on our trip.

Jet lag woke me well before light the next day to find a cold, clear morning. Walking out onto our deck, I looked at the stars and told myself, "This is where I belong. This is where I belong," trying to convince my heart to move on. Almost immediately the Lord gently corrected me. He said, "No, Kit. This isn't where you belong. This is where you live. You belong with Me. And one day you will be with Me."

If I seek to belong in this world, I will always feel out of place. My life here is just a stop on my journey toward my real home. My heart needs to be set on heaven. I live here, but I belong there.

THE LAST
leaf

"Trust in the Lord with all your heart and lean not on your own understanding; in all your ways submit to Him, and He will make your paths straight." (Proverbs 3:5-6)

Finding any leaves on the trees is hard in the middle of winter. Most of them have fallen. But some of the deciduous oaks hold on to a few leaves through winter, finally dropping them with the first warmth of spring.

As I looked out the window on a cold, clear day, a few remaining leaves drew my eye. The wind tossed the branches. At first the leaves looked as if they were enjoying being lifted into the air while still attached to the branch. But as the wind increased, the mood changed. The experience no longer looked enjoyable. The scene resembled a battle. The leaves flapped in the wind, constantly moving. They seemed to be holding on to the branch with all their strength.

Some lost their battle and became airborne. Once released, the leaves were carried wherever the wind directed. I enjoyed watching the leaves floating freely. The struggle had ended. The leaf had found its place of rest.

As I watched, the Lord reminded me of how many times I fight against the direction He gives me. Often, I ask too many questions before I obey. Or I refuse to accept the peace He offers my heart in situations I cannot control. Like the leaves that battled to hang on to their place of familiarity, I hold on tight.

When the leaf gave itself to the wind, I saw the joy of freedom. My heart longed for that freedom. But first I had my own battle to fight, the battle to let go of the known and follow God into the unknown. I must choose to obey when I can't see the outcome, and then accept the peace that only God can give in the uncontrollable situations of life.

One by one, the leaves gave me a striking visual of allowing the wind to give them freedom. One by one, I gave the Lord control over the concerns of my heart. As I did, I experienced rest in Him and the freedom for which my heart longed.

Is there a battle in your heart today? If so, may I encourage you to seek the freedom only God can offer? Then take a walk, feel the wind on your face, and enjoy knowing your concerns are in good hands.

BRIDGE
building

___

"If anyone builds on this foundation using gold, silver, costly stones, wood, hay, or straw, their work will be shown for what it is, because the Day will bring it to light. It will be revealed with fire, and the fire will test the quality of each person's work." (1 Corinthians 3:12-13)

"Building the new bridge took so long, but just a few days to destroy the old," Drew said as we drove over the new bridge, which we now take on our way to town. Well, on our way to anywhere, actually. We only have one road. Everyone out our way has enjoyed driving over the brand-new bridge that took six months to complete. It's big news for us country folks.

I had asked Drew what they would do with the old bridge. He said, "Easily tear it down." And tear it down, they did. But tearing the old bridge down took about a one-hundredth of the amount of time it took to build the new one. Therefore, Drew's comment highlighted a principle that applies to many areas of life.

The first idea that comes to mind is relationships. Good relationships with a friend, co-worker, family member, or spouse are like the new bridge. They take time and effort. Both willingness to share life together and good construction skills are needed. Unfortunately, all that progress can be quickly destroyed. Drew's comment encourages me to analyze my building methods. What do my words and actions portray? Do they build up, or do they destroy?

The second idea focuses on discipline. I've heard that changing a habit takes two weeks. I'm not sure if that is true. But I know the following to be true: a day's indiscretion can completely undermine my resolve. When I'm amid building new patterns in my life, the building seems to take forever. But the thought of a day's indiscretion undoing all my progress motivates me to maintain discipline. Building anything from a bridge to a relationship to a new habit pattern takes time—a long time. I can enhance my progress by not destroying my own efforts. How are you doing in your building skills? Do you take the time to build wisely? Sadly, tearing down will always be easier than building up.

Which brings another thought to mind: Anything worth building is worth building well.

WHICH TEAM
are you on?

———

"All the nations will be gathered before him, and he will separate the people one from another as a shepherd separates the sheep from the goats. He will put the sheep on his right and the goats on his left." Matthew (25:32-33)

I didn't excel at athletics in school. My heart would fill with dread whenever assigned a team game to play. We would line up and two students, usually the most athletic, would choose whom they wanted on their team. The team captains would take turns calling names one by one. Closer to the end than the beginning, I would hear my name. *Thank you*, my heart would silently rejoice. To be at the mercy of someone else's choice is frightening.

In Matthew 25:32-33, we see Jesus putting people into two groups, the sheep and the goats. He explains how the two groups were chosen. He reminded the first group how they had fed him, welcomed him, clothed him, and more. They asked the Lord when they had done these things. He responded, "Whatever you did for one of the least of these brothers and sisters of mine, you did for me."

The second group is also reminded of how they were chosen. They had not done anything for the least of these; thus, they had done nothing for Jesus.

Unlike in school, we can choose which team we want to be on. By faith in Jesus' death on the cross, we initially make that choice. Every time we serve in love, we reaffirm the choice to be on Jesus' team. We can be assured that we will hear Him call our name when we build a life of faith and service.

INSTANT
wisdom

"If any of you lacks wisdom, you should ask God, who gives generously to all without finding fault, and it will be given to you. But when you ask, you must believe and not doubt, because the one who doubts is like a wave of the sea, blown and tossed by the wind." (James 1:5-6)

I stood in line feeling my rights had been violated. The person in front of me had left her credit card in her car. As she went to the parking lot, I asked the clerk if she could check me out. Her answer: "No." I tried to get out of the line, but others waited behind me. I was trapped. So I waited impatiently for what seemed like the better part of my morning but was probably only a few minutes.

Possibly you have been in that situation, or one similar. Our culture—which I unfortunately reflect all too often—has lost the ability to wait for anything. Patience is a virtue of the past. If you don't think you have been affected, wait in line today. Any line will do.

There are many troubling consequences from our inability to wait. One that I'm learning about is the area of wisdom. Wisdom is mentioned 218 times in the scriptures (NIV). Wise is mentioned 182 times, and there are five books of the Bible that are considered Wisdom Literature. Wisdom is something we are told to strive for and obtain. But I think we have distorted the means to acquiring wisdom because of our demand for instant gratification.

Some would say all you have to do is ask and wisdom will be granted. Like rubbing a bottle, the genie comes out to do your bidding. While I believe that on occasion God will give us "wisdom" for a crisis situation that is more of a directive, an answer for that situation, true wisdom comes with pursuit. And pursuit takes time and effort.

I am not a theologian, but James 1:5-6 has taken on a new meaning to me. Why the mention of doubting if God gives wisdom generously and without reproach? One of the reasons I believe is because we are going to have to wait as wisdom is developed in us. And as we wait, we are reminded to not doubt. To me these verses reflect our ability or inability to trust God as He reveals His wisdom over time.

Have you been asking for wisdom? I have, for over a year. Have I been given wisdom? Yes, partially, as I have pursued wisdom by making phone calls, doing research, talking with Drew and others I trust. All of these should fill our time as we wait. Remember, wisdom is a pursuit. It is active.

I have been overwhelmed at times questioning the certainty of receiving the wisdom I need. When that happens, I have reminded myself to trust God. He will give me the wisdom I seek. My story has not ended yet. But through my active pursuit of wisdom and learning to trust God over time, I'm being changed.

THE BEGINNING OF
abundance

———

I began this mini-book with the idea of abundance and the desire to share the abundant goodness of God to me over my lifetime. But there were also years of my life before I knew God's abundance.

Those years weren't remarkable in any way. But there was an emptiness in my life I couldn't seem to leave behind me. The pursuit of trying to fill the emptiness took many forms. However, none were successful.

I had been raised with a foundation of spiritual principles. I believed there was a God. I believed Jesus Christ was the Son of God. I knew I was a sinner. And I even believed Jesus died on the cross to pay the penalty for my sins. But none of that seemed to fill the emptiness in my life until one night when I was invited to personally accept God's gift of salvation.

Through praying a prayer much like the one below I went from an intellectual belief in spiritual principles to receiving forgiveness and beginning a relationship with a merciful God who wanted me to experience His love and plan for my life.

My prayer was something like this: "Jesus, I need you. I know I have chosen to go my own way and have sinned against you. Please forgive me. I want to know you personally. I want to live a life that will please you. I know I cannot do that on my own. I need you to live your life through me. I give you my life."

At the end of my prayer my life changed forever. My spiritual life went from vague principles I had learned as a child to a relationship with God who loved me. And more importantly, God wanted to be a part of my life. He filled the emptiness my heart had known for so long. His abundance was beginning in my life and has continued to this day.

If you do not have a personal relationship with God, please consider beginning one today. My prayer for you is that you also would know God's love, forgiveness, and plan for your life.

"Grace and peace be yours in abundance through the knowledge of God and of Jesus our Lord." (2 Peter 1:2)

What is a
more than ordinary life?

Each person's life is unique and special. In that sense, there is no such thing as an ordinary life. However, many people yearn for lives more special: excitement, adventure, romance, purpose, character. Our site is dedicated to the premise that any life can be more than ordinary.

At **MoreThanOrdinaryLives.com** you will find:

- inspiring stories
- ideas and resources
- entertaining novels
- free downloads

https://morethanordinarylives.com/

Challenge Series

by Kit and Drew Coons

Challenge for Two
Book One

A series of difficult circumstances have forced Dave and Katie Parker into early retirement. Searching for new life and purpose, the Parkers take a wintertime job house sitting an old Victorian mansion. The picturesque river town in southeastern Minnesota is far from the climate and culture of their home near the Alabama Gulf Coast.

But dark secrets sleep in the mansion. A criminal network has ruthlessly intimidated the community since the timber baron era of the 19th century. Residents have been conditioned to look the other way.

The Parkers' questions about local history and clues they discover in the mansion bring an evil past to light and create division in the small community. While some fear the consequences of digging up the truth, others want freedom from crime and justice for victims. Faced with personal threats, the Parkers must decide how to respond for themselves and for the good of the community.

Challenge Down Under
Book Two

Dave and Katie Parker's only son, Jeremy, is getting married in Australia. In spite of initial reservations, the Parkers discover that Denyse is perfect for Jeremy and that she's the daughter they've always wanted. But she brings with her a colorful and largely dysfunctional Aussie family. Again Dave and Katie are fish out of water as they try to relate to a boisterous clan in a culture very different from their home in South Alabama.

After the wedding, Denyse feels heartbroken that her younger brother, Trevor, did not attend. Details emerge that lead Denyse to believe her brother may be in trouble. Impressed by his parents' sleuthing experience in Minnesota, Jeremy volunteers them to locate Trevor. Their search leads them on an adventure through Australia and New Zealand.

Unfortunately, others are also searching for Trevor, with far more sinister intentions. With a talent for irresponsible chicanery inherited from his family, Trevor has left a trail of trouble in his wake and has been forced into servitude. Can Dave and Katie locate him in time?

Challenge in Mobile
Book Three

Dave and Katie Parker regret that their only child Jeremy, his wife Denyse, and their infant daughter live on the opposite side of the world. Unexpectedly, Jeremy calls to ask his father's help finding an accounting job in the US. Katie urges Dave to do whatever is necessary to find a job for Jeremy near Mobile. Dave's former accounting firm has floundered since his departure. The Parkers risk their financial security by purchasing full ownership of the struggling firm to make a place for Jeremy.

Denyse finds South Alabama fascinating compared to her native Australia. She quickly resumes her passion for teaching inner-city teenagers. Invited by Katie, other colorful guests arrive from Australia and Minnesota to experience Gulf Coast culture. Aided by their guests, Dave and Katie examine their faith after Katie receives discouraging news from her doctors.

Political, financial, and racial tensions have been building in Mobile. Bewildering financial expenditures of a client create suspicions of criminal activity. Denyse hears disturbing rumors from her students. A hurricane from the Gulf of Mexico exacerbates the community's tensions. Dave and Katie are pulled into a crisis that requires them to rise to a new level of more than ordinary.

More from Kit and Drew Coons

The Ambassadors

Two genetically engineered beings unexpectedly arrive on Earth. Unlike most extraterrestrials depicted in science fiction, the pair is attractive, personable, and telegenic—the perfect talk show guests. They have come to Earth as ambassadors bringing an offer of partnership in a confederation of civilizations. Technological advances are offered as part of the partnership. But humans must learn to cooperate among themselves to join.

Molly, a young reporter, and Paul, a NASA scientist, have each suffered personal tragedy and carry emotional baggage. They are asked to tutor the ambassadors in human ways and to guide them on a worldwide goodwill tour. Molly and Paul observe as the extraterrestrials commit faux pas while experiencing human culture. They struggle trying to define a romance and partnership while dealing with burdens of the past.

However, mankind finds implementing actual change difficult. Clashing value systems and conflicts among subgroups of humanity erupt. Inevitably, rather than face difficult choices, fearmongers in the media start to blame the messengers. Then an uncontrolled biological weapon previously created by a rogue country tips the world into chaos. Molly, Paul, and the others must face complex moral decisions about what being human means and the future of mankind.

MINI SERIES

More Than Ordinary Challenges—
Dealing with the Unexpected

More Than Ordinary Marriage—
A Higher Level

More Than Ordinary Faith—
Why Does God Allow Suffering?

More Than Ordinary Wisdom—
Stories of Faith and Folly

More Than Ordinary Abundance—
From Kit's Heart

More Than Ordinary Choices—
Making Good Decisions

Visit **https://morethanordinarylives.com/**
for more information.

About the Authors

Kit and Drew Coons met while Christian missionaries in Africa in 1980. As humorous speakers specializing in strengthening relationships, they have taught in every part of the US and in thirty-nine other countries. For two years, the Coonses lived and served in New Zealand and Australia. They are keen cultural observers and incorporate their many adventures into their writing. Kit and Drew are unique in that they speak and write as a team.

55029459R00046

Made in the USA
Columbia, SC
08 April 2019